T0344147

# THE A-Z OF PRIMARY TEACHING

## 200+ TERMS EVERY NEW PRIMARY TEACHER NEEDS TO KNOW

## REBECCA AUSTIN AND JUSTINE EARL

Learning Matters

Learning Matters
A SAGE Publishing Company
1 Oliver's Yard
55 City Road
London EC1Y 1SP

SAGE Publications Inc.
2455 Teller Road
Thousand Oaks, California 91320

SAGE Publications India Pvt Ltd
B 1/I 1 Mohan Cooperative Industrial Area
Mathura Road
New Delhi 110 044

SAGE Publications Asia-Pacific Pte Ltd
3 Church Street
#10-04 Samsung Hub
Singapore 049483

Editor: Amy Thornton
Senior project editor: Chris Marke
Project management: River Editorial
Cover design: Wendy Scott
Typeset by: C&M Digitals (P) Ltd, Chennai, India
Printed in the UK

**Library of Congress Control Number: 2022933434**

**British Library Cataloguing in Publication Data**

A catalogue record for this book is available
from the British Library

ISBN 978-1-5297-7986-8
ISBN 978-1-5297-7985-1 (pbk)

At SAGE we take sustainability seriously. Most of our products are printed in the UK using responsibly sourced
papers and boards. When we print overseas we ensure sustainable papers are used as measured by the
PREPS grading system. We undertake an annual audit to monitor our sustainability.

# CONTENTS

Contents

# ABOUT THE AUTHORS

**Rebecca Austin** is Senior Lecturer and Primary English Team Leader at Canterbury Christ Church University. Rebecca teaches on primary English courses across a range of initial teacher education programmes, as well as at master's and doctoral level. She also provides staff development for schools in relation to primary English and learning outside the classroom.

In addition to primary English, Rebecca's interests are: the role of parents in children's education, including the role of homework; the identity of learners in schools; learning outside the classroom; media education in primary schools; and alternative research methodologies.

**Justine Earl** has been a teacher educator for over two decades, as an advisory teacher and as a Senior Lecturer in Primary Education. Over her time as a university tutor, Justine has been a Faculty Lead for Partnerships and a Programme Director for the PGCE primary part-time route. Justine also worked on the Teach First programme, supporting participants in the classroom, guiding their academic work and delivering professional development in English.

Justine spent many years as a primary class teacher. She has continued working on developing school partnerships and supporting schools with research and development projects, as well as other CPD. She is a qualified coach and has an interest in coaching and mentoring in educational settings.

# ABOUT THIS BOOK

If you are new to the world of education, it can be a real challenge to get to grips with the terminology that you will come across every day. There are technical terms, countless acronyms and even everyday words which have a very specific meaning in the context of a school or classroom.

When you need to be able to find out quickly and easily what it is that everyone is talking about, you can turn to this book. The succinct definitions enable you to tune into the general area of discussion and provide the basis for exploring things in more depth.

Entries are organised alphabetically and linked to other relevant terms and definitions. If you prefer, you can go straight to the list of acronyms before looking at the accompanying definition.

For student teachers, this book can be your way into the language of education for both your studies and your practical teaching experiences. For early career teachers, you can use it to check up on your knowledge in school – so that you sail through staff meetings with ease!

School governors and parents might also find it useful to enable you to engage in conversations and meetings more confidently.

Rebecca Austin and Justine Earl

# ABILITY GROUPING

An approach to teaching which involves seating children in the classroom with others of similar ability and providing work that is differentiated (see **differentiation**) to the different abilities.

# ABSTRACT THINKING

Being able to use metaphors and analogies to understand ideas that do not have a physical representation in the world. Babies and children move from **concrete thinking** to abstract thinking as they develop, and teachers can help this through the examples they use in their teaching.

# ACADEMY

A **state school** that is not under **local authority (LA)** control, but which is funded directly from the government and has the status of an **independent school**. Academies have greater freedoms than LA schools in relation to how they run. For example, they do not have to follow the **national curriculum** or the **school teachers' pay and conditions document (STPCD)**. Schools can opt to become an academy; if **Ofsted** judges an LA maintained school to be inadequate, it *must* become an academy. Academies are run by an **academy trust**.

# ACADEMY TRUST

A not-for-profit organisation which runs an academy or group/chain of academies. Individual trustees will play a similar role to that of school governors on the **school governing body**. Academy trusts might be sponsored by a business, organisation or voluntary group. These sponsors support the work of the trust.

See also **Multi-Academy Trust (MAT)**.

# ACTION RESEARCH

An approach to research which identifies an issue in the classroom, implements an approach to tackle the issue and collects data to ascertain its effectiveness. It is often seen as a cyclical approach as the findings suggest actions which then feed back into classroom practice; the results of this are then evaluated and further changes to practice implemented.

## ADAPTIVE TEACHING

Using teaching approaches which are designed to support learners based on their particular learning needs. Includes providing targeted support during lessons. See also **differentiation**.

# ADDITIONAL EDUCATIONAL NEEDS (AEN)

Any need which has an effect on children's learning in school, but which falls outside of the needs described as **special educational needs (SEN)**.

## ANALYTIC PHONICS

An approach to teaching phonics that identifies similarities between strings of letters in words which represent a particular 'rime'. For example, children would be taught words such as *night, fright, sight, light* together and taught to identify the 'ight' string as a consistent spelling pattern. The 'rime' is the string of letters following and including the first vowel in a word (*ight* in the above examples) and the 'onset' is the letters preceding the first vowel (n, fr, s, l respectively in the above examples).

# ANNUAL REVIEW

A meeting held annually to review the **statement of special educational needs** or **education, health and care plan (EHCP)** to ascertain whether the provision in place for the child is meeting their needs appropriately or not.

## APPROPRIATE BODIES

An organisation such as a **local authority (LA)** which quality assures the induction period of **early career teachers (ECTs)**.

# ASSESSMENT

Any activity or process that is used to check on progress in learning. Two main types of assessment are **formative assessment** and **summative assessment**.

# ASSESSMENT FOR LEARNING (AFL)

See **formative assessment**.

# ASSESSMENT ONLY (AO)

The assessment only route to gaining **qualified teacher status (QTS)** is open to those who can demonstrate that they already meet the **teachers' standards** without the need for further training. They must present detailed evidence, and this and their teaching is reviewed and assessed in a school by an accredited provider.

# ASSISTANT HEAD TEACHER (AHT)

A member of the **senior leadership team**.

# ATTACHMENT DISORDER

Children can have difficulty establishing a deep emotional connection (the attachment bond) with a parent or caregiver, resulting in emotional and behavioural problems. There are two recognised types of attachment disorder: reactive (RAD) and disinhibited, or disinhibited social engagement disorder (DSED).

# ATTAINMENT

Children's level of achievement as measured by tests or other **summative assessments**.

# ATTAINMENT GAP

The gap in attainment between different groups of children. For example, boys and girls or those from ethnic minorities or from different socio-economic backgrounds (see also **closing the gap**).

## ATTAINMENT SCORES

Children's attainment as measured by **standardised assessment tasks (SATs)** at the end of **Key Stage 1** and **Key Stage 2**.

## ATTENTION DEFICIT HYPERACTIVITY DISORDER (ADHD)

A neurodevelopmental disorder. Refers to a pattern of behaviour that affects a child in most situations. It begins early in a child's life and can continue into adulthood. Children with ADHD often find it difficult to concentrate, can be hyperactive and may act impulsively. It is highly likely that a child with ADHD will have at least one other condition, such as a social communication disorder, **dyslexia** or dyspraxia.

## AUTISTIC SPECTRUM DISORDER (ASD)

The medical name for autism.

# ADD ANY MORE DEFINITIONS YOU LEARN HERE...

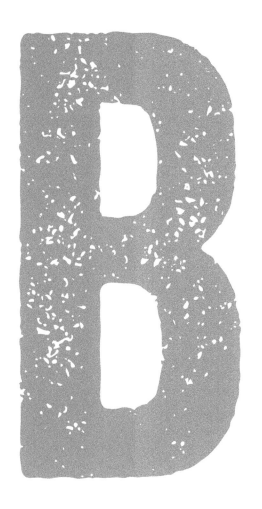

# BAKER DAYS

See **in service training days**.

# BASELINE ASSESSMENT

See **reception baseline assessment (RBA)**.

# BEHAVIOUR FOR LEARNING (B4L)

The desired behaviour that enables children to participate in learning and learn effectively. Rather than a purely disciplinary approach, a B4L approach considers the needs of individual children and the potential barriers to learning and attempts to find ways to support children to regulate their own behaviour effectively. From work by Simon Ellis and Janet Tod.

# BEHAVIOURISM

A **learning theory** that suggests that children adapt their behaviour in relation to rewards and sanctions. The use of praise and rewards such as stickers comes from a behaviourist approach.

# BEHAVIOUR MANAGEMENT (BM)

The strategies, approaches and ethos by which schools and teachers manage the behaviour of children in the classroom and school. See also **behaviour for learning (B4L)**.

# BEHAVIOUR SUPPORT PLAN (BSP)

A plan put in place by the school to support children with behavioural difficulties that are affecting their ability to engage in learning in the classroom.

## BENCHMARKING

A process by which standards are agreed for assessments in relation to age or other criteria - see also **moderation**.

## BLACK ASIAN AND MINORITY ETHNIC (BAME)

A term that can include several ethnic groups. In March 2021, the Commission on Race and Ethnic Disparities recommended that the government stop using the term BAME. This term might still be used in schools.

## BRITISH EDUCATION RESEARCH ASSOCIATION (BERA)

Promotes research in all aspects of education and provides a forum to disseminate and discuss research findings through publications and conferences.

# ADD ANY MORE DEFINITIONS YOU LEARN HERE...

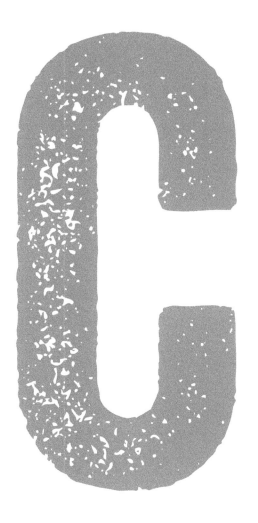

# CAMBRIDGE PRIMARY REVIEW (CPR)

A comprehensive independent inquiry into primary education. The final report *Children, their World, their Education* was published in 2009. Now known as the Cambridge Primary Review Trust (CPRT).

## CATCH-UP PREMIUM: CORONAVIRUS COVID-19

One-off special funding for non-independent schools to support children and young people to catch up on missed learning due to the impact of the coronavirus (COVID-19). Schools must publish on their websites how they use the funding.

# CHAIR OF GOVERNORS

Heads up a **school governing body**.

## CHARTERED COLLEGE OF TEACHING (CCT)

The professional body for teachers. A repository of research and resources to support teaching. Provides a platform for teachers' voices to be heard. Membership is free to student teachers but requires a subscription once teachers are qualified.

# CHILD AND ADOLESCENT MENTAL HEALTH SERVICES (CAMHS)

Work with children and young people who are struggling with their mental health. Also provide support for families and carers.

## CHILD-CENTRED

An approach to teaching and learning that focuses on children's interests, needs and developmental stage rather than external criteria or curriculum requirements.

# CHILD IN CARE (CIC)

A child in the care of the **local authority (LA)**. Also known as a **looked after child (LAC)** or child looked after (CLA).

# CHILD PROTECTION (CP)

The actions that are taken to protect children from significant harm. The role of the **designated safeguarding lead (DSL)** includes child protection.

# CHILDREN AND FAMILIES ACT (CFA)

A 2014 law relating to the support provided for children with **special educational needs and disabilities (SEND)**.

# CLOSING THE GAP

A term used to describe how schools are approaching differences in assessment outcomes for groups of children. For example, the gap between outcomes for boys and girls, for children from different ethnic groups, or children from different socio-economic backgrounds.

# COACHING

In education, coaching is less directive than **mentoring**. A coach will facilitate the growth of the teacher or trainee/student teacher through supporting their self-reflection and development. In **ITT/ITE**, a mentor will use a range of mentoring and coaching strategies when working with beginner teachers.

# COASTING SCHOOLS

Schools that have high **attainment and progress scores** but are not showing year on year improvement.

# COGNITIVE LOAD

Describes how information from the working memory can become overloaded and requires that learners have processed and stored information in the long-term memory in order to be able to learn effectively.

# COGNITIVE SCIENCE

The study of intelligence and how the mind works. Draws on a range of disciplines such as psychology, philosophy and **neuroscience**, among others.

# COMBINED SCORES

The combined attainment outcomes for children in maths, reading and writing. See also **progress scores** and **attainment scores**.

# COMMON ASSESSMENT FRAMEWORK (CAF)

A framework for assessing the needs of families and children so that the appropriate agencies can be deployed to best support them. Being replaced by the 'the early help assessment'.

# CONCRETE THINKING

Thinking that relates to what can be observed, touched and interacted with in the physical world. As they learn, children move from concrete to **abstract thinking** and teachers will provide both concrete and abstract examples in teaching in order to move children's learning on.

# CONSTRUCTIVISM

A **learning theory** that suggests that we learn by building on what we already know and can do and there are predictable developmental stages that all learners go through, which can be planned for in teaching ideas and concepts.

# CONTINUING PROFESSIONAL DEVELOPMENT (CPD)

Supports teachers in developing skills and knowledge and aims to enhance practice. CPD activities can include: **coaching**; **mentoring**; **team teaching**; lesson observation and feedback; **lesson study**; sharing good practice opportunities; training sessions; conferences; networking meetings; visits to other schools; **postgraduate** study; teachers researching their practice; international visits and exchanges.

Schools have five days per year set aside for 'in service training and education' – **INSET days** – these are used for CPD activities.

CPD for new teachers is through the **early career framework (ECF)**.

CPD can also support career progression; for example, from middle to senior leadership.

# CORE CONTENT FRAMEWORK (CCF)

Also referred to as initial teacher training core content framework (ITTCCF).

A 2019 policy document that sets out what trainee teachers should experience during **initial teacher training (ITT)**. Universities and the schools they work with use the CCF to design and deliver their ITT programmes. This framework leads into the **early career framework**.

# CORE SUBJECTS

Usually refers to English, mathematics and science in primary schools.

# CURRICULUM

Can be defined as the subjects offered/studied in a school, as well as the detail of each of the subjects (e.g. 'the history curriculum'). More broadly, it can be used to mean all the activities that take place in the context of a school. See also **hidden curriculum**.

# ADD ANY MORE DEFINITIONS YOU LEARN HERE...

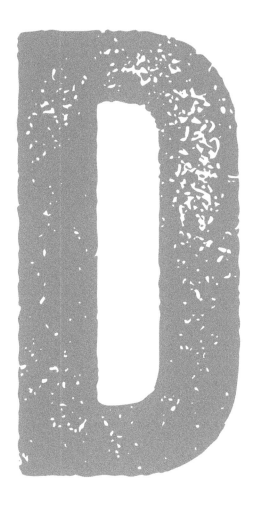

# DEEP DIVE

A focused evaluation of a subject as part of an Ofsted inspection. In Primary inspections following the 2019 Inspection Framework, there will always be a deep dive into reading as well as one or two foundation subjects and sometimes mathematics.

## DEPARTMENT FOR EDUCATION (DFE)

The ministerial department of the government responsible for children's services and education, including Early Years, schools, higher and further education, apprenticeships and wider skills in England. Scotland, Wales and Northern Ireland have their own education departments and different policies.

Past names for this department:

In 1992, the Department for Education and Science was renamed the Department for Education (DfE).

In 1995, the department merged with the Department for Employment to become the Department for Education and Employment (DfEE).

In 2001, it was renamed the Department for Education and Skills (DfES).

In 2007, it became the Department for Children, Schools and Families (DCSF), changing to the DfE in 2010.

It is important to note which name is used when reading about education policy, statutory guidance and law, as this indicates the political party in power at that time.

## DEPUTY HEAD TEACHER (DHT)

One or more teachers who are second in seniority in the **senior leadership team (SLT)**.

## DESIGNATED SAFEGUARDING LEAD (DSL)

The member of senior school staff who has responsibility for all matters of safeguarding and child protection. Safeguarding concerns are reported to the DSL. The DSL liaises with the **local authority designated officer (LADO)** on aspects of child protection, as well as with external safeguarding agencies where required, such as social services and the police.

# DEVELOPMENTAL LANGUAGE DISORDER (DLD)

Children with DLD have difficulties with language that persist throughout their lives. DLD affects approximately two children in each average primary class of 30 children in the UK. The difficulties are separate to conditions such as autism, hearing impairment, genetic disorders or neurodegenerative conditions. However, DLD can co-occur with other difficulties.

# DEVELOPMENT MATTERS

Non-statutory guidance for practitioners following the **Early Years Foundation Stage (EYFS)**.

# DIDACTIC

A teaching approach in which teachers deliver input to learners and there is little or no interaction. Might also be known as 'chalk and talk'.

# DIFFERENTIATION

Adjusting a lesson to meet the needs of different learners. This might be done by providing different or extra learning resources for specific children or groups of children; by having different expected outcomes for some children; or by providing additional targeted support from the teacher, teaching assistant or other adult.

Differentiation might also involve **ability grouping**.

This might also be referred to as **adaptive** and/or **inclusive teaching**.

# DIRECTED ACTIVITIES RELATED TO TEXTS (DARTS)

Activities to support children's comprehension of and engagement with texts - rather than a list of questions to answer.

# DIRECTED TIME

Time when a teacher must be available to carry out duties under the direction of the head teacher, including meetings, PPA time, morning and afternoon breaks, parent/carer consultations and training days. This is a maximum of 1265 hours in a school year.

## DISCLOSURE AND BARRING SERVICE (DBS)

The service that helps employers make safer recruitment decisions by processing and issuing DBS checks for all those who wish to work with children or vulnerable adults. It also makes decisions as to whether an individual should be included on a list banning them from engaging in roles working with children or vulnerable adults.

# DIVERSITY

Refers to the various ways in which people, their identities, their circumstances, their worldviews and their experiences differ from each other. In education, there is a commitment to ensuring that these differences are respected, valued and represented within the curriculum and in teaching and learning contexts in school. See also **inclusion**.

## DOMAIN-SPECIFIC KNOWLEDGE

**Subject knowledge** which is specifically related to a particular subject or 'domain'.

# DUAL CODING

Providing two different representations of the same information to help children understand it. Careful combinations of words and images are needed to make this effective. Meaningful combinations of pictures, diagrams, visual organisers and words are used. Dual coding may be used in the creation of **knowledge organisers**.

## DUTY OF CARE

Teachers, including those who are training, have a duty of care towards children. This is part of a teacher's legal responsibilities. This means they must apply their education and skills to safeguard children. Their actions must be those of a reasonable person in the circumstances of class teaching. The duty of care to individual children needs to take into account factors including age, health and the educational context. Teachers must act in accordance with school procedures, policies and guidelines.

## DYSLEXIA

A learning difficulty related to learning to read and spell. It might also affect other information processing and organisational skills.

# ADD ANY MORE DEFINITIONS YOU LEARN HERE...

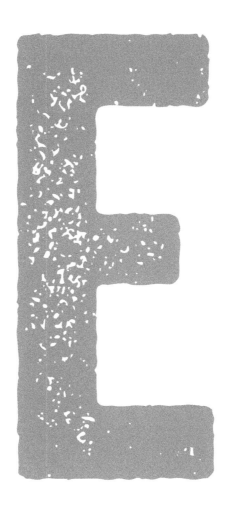

# EARLY CAREER FRAMEWORK (ECF)

Used to support newly qualified teachers in the first two years of teaching. It outlines the support available to them and is focused on professional development in teaching, subject knowledge and managing workload. It builds on the **core content framework (CCF)**.

# EARLY CAREER TEACHER (ECT)

A teacher in their first two years of teaching. They are entitled to support through the **early career framework**. Previously a teacher in their first year of teaching was known as a newly qualified teacher (NQT).

# EARLY LEARNING GOALS

Achievement and development goals set out in the EYFS. Progress towards these goals is used to complete the **Early Years Foundation Stage Profile**.

# EARLY YEARS FOUNDATION STAGE (EYFS)

Sets out the standards for development and learning and care for children from birth to five. Used in all pre-school care and learning settings and reception classes in primary schools. Sometimes referred to as the **Foundation Stage (FS)**. Supported by **development matters**.

# EARLY YEARS FOUNDATION STAGE PROFILE

A summary of a child's achievement and progress at the end of the **Early Years Foundation Stage** (the end of the Reception Year in primary schools).

# EARLY YEARS TEACHER STATUS

Graduates working in an Early Years setting can receive training to meet specially adapted **teachers' standards** (teachers' standards (Early Years)). If successful, trainees are awarded Early Years teacher status. This is not, however, a qualification that confers **QTS**.

# EDUCATIONAL PSYCHOLOGIST (EP)

Assesses children with learning, social, emotional or behavioural difficulties and recommends how children might be supported in schools.

# EDUCATION ENDOWMENT FOUNDATION (EEF)

A charity set up in 2011 by the Sutton Trust with the aim of breaking the link between family income and educational achievement. It is one of nine centres in the government's 'What Works Network'. It generates evidence by working with schools on research as well as providing the **EEF teaching and learning toolkit** of research.

# EDUCATION, HEALTH AND CARE PLAN (EHCP)

An official document for children and young people aged up to 25 who require support. It identifies their educational, health and social needs and the additional support required to meet those needs. There is a specific process to go through to apply for an EHCP and not all applications are agreed. Once in place, it is legally binding. Introduced in September 2014 to replace the **statement of special educational needs**. The latter led to children being referred to as 'statemented children' – a term that might still be used in schools.

# EDUCATION WELFARE OFFICER (EWO)

Employed by local councils to ensure all children attend school full-time and support schools and families to make this happen.

# EEF TEACHING AND LEARNING TOOLKIT

Summarises many pieces of academic research and indicates the strength of the evidence, the impact of the research findings and the cost of implementation to support decisions about different approaches that might be taken in schools.

# EMOTIONAL INTELLIGENCE

A person's ability to understand, monitor and regulate their own emotions. Based on work by Daniel Goleman.

## THE ENGAGEMENT MODEL

From September 2021, used to make assessments of children working below the standard of national curriculum tests. Likely to be used with children with profound learning needs. See also **pre-key stage standards**.

# ENGLISH AS AN ADDITIONAL LANGUAGE (EAL)

This refers to a child whose first language is other than English. A child may be able to communicate in more than one language, which is why this term replaced the use of English as a second language (ESL). If a child acquires English subsequent to their first language development, then English is an additional language even if they become highly proficient in it. It is very important to know the languages that children speak and those that are spoken at home, as well as knowing if a child is literate in a language or languages other than English.

## ENGLISH HUBS

Introduced in 2018, these are schools with excellent practice in the teaching of reading and phonics who provide advice, guidance and support to schools in the surrounding area. Hubs are identified and funded by the **DfE**.

# EQUALITY AND HUMAN RIGHTS COMMISSION (EHRC)

Works to safeguard and uphold laws relating to equality and human rights and discrimination.

# EVEN BETTER IF (EBI)

This might be a marking comment made by a teacher to support a child in making the next steps in their learning. Often used with **what went well (WWW)**.

# EVIDENCE-BASED TEACHING (EBT)

Drawing on evidence from educational research and cognitive science to inform approaches to teaching.

# EXCLUSION

A measure which can be taken to exclude a child from attending school - this might be a fixed period exclusion for up to 45 days, or a permanent exclusion. Children who are excluded may be educated in a **pupil referral unit (PRU)** if the exclusion is for longer than five days.

# EXPOSITION

A clear and detailed explanation and the act of providing such an explanation.

# EXTRINSIC MOTIVATION

To be motivated by an external factor, such as a reward or praise.

# ADD ANY MORE DEFINITIONS YOU LEARN HERE...

# FAMILY LIAISON OFFICER (FLO)

The person in school who provides pastoral support to parent/carers, providing information and education as well as liaising with local authorities and other agencies. Can support parents through child protection issues and meetings. This role involves home visits.

# FEEDBACK

Information given in a range of ways to a learner about their performance. Might be verbal or written (e.g. through marking children's work).

# FEMALE GENITAL MUTILATION (FGM)

A form of child abuse that is illegal in the UK. It involves the unnecessary cutting of the genitals of young girls. Teachers are required to undertake training that supports them to be alert to signs that children they work with might be at risk of FGM. Known cases must be reported to the police. In secondary schools, it is now compulsory to teach children about FGM as a form of abuse, as part of the **RSE** curriculum.

# FIXED MINDSET

See **growth mindset**.

# FLOOR STANDARD

The minimum expectation for attainment and progress by children in a school.

# FLUENCY

In reading, this is being able to read accurately and with appropriate pace and expression. It may also be applied to mathematics where it refers to children being able to apply fundamental maths knowledge and skills adaptably across a range of contexts.

# FOREST SCHOOL

Where a regular part of the school curriculum is dedicated to children's learning outdoors. It is underpinned by a child-centred, play-based approach to interacting with natural settings. This might be affiliated with the official forest school organisation or a part of a more general outdoor learning policy.

# FORMATIVE ASSESSMENT

**Assessments** that are used to feed into the next steps in learning. They usually assess learning over a short timeframe (e.g. within the context of one lesson). Formative assessment might involve questioning children, marking work, observation, etc. Also known as **assessment for learning (AfL)**.

# FOUNDATION STAGE (FS)

See **Early Years Foundation Stage (EYFS)**.

# FOUNDATION SUBJECTS

Usually: geography, history, music, physical education, design technology, computing, art, primary languages. Religious education is sometimes referred to as a foundation subject although technically it has the same status as the **core subjects**, which are compulsory for all children.

# FREE SCHOOL MEALS (FSM)

A lunch provided free to eligible children. Families who are on low incomes and/or receiving certain benefits can register for free school meals for their children.

# FREE SCHOOLS

Free schools are like **academies**, but they are new schools rather than schools that started as **maintained schools** and converted to academy status. Free schools are independent schools as they receive their funding direct from the government, but they are still **state schools** as they do not charge fees.

# FUNDAMENTAL BRITISH VALUES (FBVS) (ALSO REFERRED TO AS BASIC BRITISH VALUES OR BRITISH VALUES)

All independent and state-maintained schools have a duty to actively promote the fundamental British values of: democracy; the rule of law; individual liberty and mutual respect and tolerance of those with different faiths and beliefs. These values were first set out by the government in 2011 as part of the **prevent strategy**.

## FUNDAMENTAL ENGLISH AND MATHEMATICS

**Initial teacher training** providers must make an assessment of a trainee's/ student teacher's knowledge and use of English and mathematics before an award of **qualified teacher status** or **Early Years teacher status** can be made. Different providers will go about assessing relevant skills and knowledge in different ways. These will include providing audits and self-study resources, administering tests and evaluating the use of written English in tasks and academic work, as well as the use of spoken English and mathematical knowledge in lessons.

# ADD ANY MORE DEFINITIONS YOU LEARN HERE...

# GIFTED AND TALENTED (G&T)

A term that was used in schools to recognise children who excelled in one or more areas of the curriculum. The G&T programme is no longer in place, but the government recommends that **pupil premium (PP)** funding might be used to support highly able students from disadvantaged backgrounds.

## GRAMMAR, PUNCTUATION AND SPELLING (GPS)

Also known as **spelling, punctuation and grammar (SPaG)**. Aspects of writing that are tested as part of the statutory end of Key Stage 2 **SATs**.

# GRAPHEME

See **systematic synthetic phonics (SSP)**.

## GRAPHEME-PHONEME CORRESPONDENCE (GPC)

See **systematic synthetic phonics (SSP)**.

# GREATER DEPTH

Used in assessments in schools to indicate children who have met the national curriculum expectations for their attainment and who have moved on to develop greater depth of understanding of the aspects covered. See also **working at the expected standard** and **working towards the expected standard**.

## GROWTH MINDSET

An approach to teaching and feedback that encourages teachers and children to see the potential for future development in an area of work even if this is not achievable yet. This avoids a focus on 'failure' in the present as being indicative of future failure (a **fixed mindset**). From work by Carol Dweck.

# GUIDED READING

An approach to reading based on work by Irene Fountas and Gay Su Pinnell. It involves children developing independent reading skills of decoding and comprehension through engaging with a carefully chosen text that can be used to teach specific skills to a group of children with similar needs.

Some schools have started to adapt this approach for use with whole classes – this is based on a different set of principles.

# ADD ANY MORE DEFINITIONS YOU LEARN HERE...

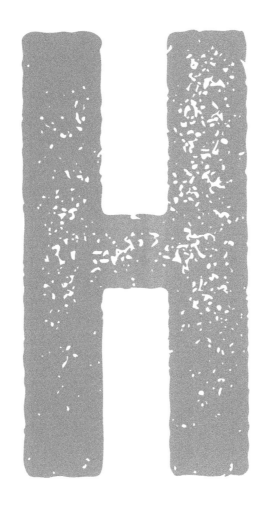

# HEARING IMPAIRMENT (HI)

A disability related to hearing difficulties.

## HER MAJESTY'S CHIEF INSPECTOR OF SCHOOLS (HMCI)

The Chief Inspector heads up **Ofsted**.

# HER MAJESTY'S INSPECTORATE (HMI)/HER MAJESTY'S INSPECTORS (HMIS)

Train, monitor and advise Ofsted inspectors. An HMI might be the lead inspector in an Ofsted inspection.

## HIDDEN CURRICULUM

What children learn in school that is not part of the official curriculum. This includes attitudes, beliefs, behaviours and values. These are likely to be implicit in the way that the school is run and therefore might not be explicitly examined in the school context.

# HIGHER LEVEL TEACHING ASSISTANT (HLTA)

An education support role where the assistant takes responsibility for learning activities under an agreed system of supervision. This can involve planning, preparation and delivery of learning for individuals, groups or, on a short time basis, the whole class. HLTAs may monitor and assess children, as well as record and report on achievement, progress and development.

## HOME SCHOOLING

When parents choose to educate their children at home and do not send them to school. Also called elective home education.

# ADD ANY MORE DEFINITIONS YOU LEARN HERE...

# INCLUSION

In education, this refers to the practice of enabling all children to work together in a school or classroom regardless of any **special educational needs** or disability, or other characteristic that might lead to them being marginalised or excluded.

# INCLUSIVE TEACHING

The practice of including all children in all lessons through the provision of appropriate support and acknowledgement of where differences might affect children's opportunities to engage and succeed in lessons.

See also **adaptive teaching**, **differentiation** and **intervention groups**.

# INDEPENDENT SCHOOLS

Are independent of government (including **local authority**) control. May be fee-paying, but might also be government funded e.g. an **academy**.

# INDIVIDUAL EDUCATION PLAN (IEP)

Sets out the goals and targets for a child during a school year along with the support required. Schools can produce IEPs for any child, but they might be used as an interim measure while an **education, health and care plan (EHCP)** is being put in place.

# INITIAL TEACHER TRAINING (ITT)

Also known as initial teacher education (ITE) or initial teacher training and education (ITTE). The period of training/study before gaining **qualified teacher status (QTS)**. Those working towards **QTS** are known as **trainee teachers**, **student teachers** or **pre-service teachers**. The latter term is more common outside of the UK.

# IN SERVICE TRAINING DAYS (INSET)

**Maintained schools** are required to include five days each year that are set aside for staff training and development, and which are not attended by children. Schools can decide when these days will be and what the focus will be. Other schools, such as **academies**, can decide how many INSET days to hold each year.

These days were introduced in 1988 by the then Secretary of State for Education, Kenneth Baker, so are sometimes called **Baker days**.

# INSTITUTE OF TEACHING

From 2022, this will provide **initial teacher training (ITT)** and **continuing professional development (CPD)** for teachers and leaders.

# INTERLEAVING

An approach to teaching that requires learners to switch between different concepts and ideas while learning; for example, alternating between concrete and abstract examples to develop depth of understanding.

# INTERVENTION GROUPS

The practice of teaching groups of children outside the classroom in order to support them with a particular aspect of the curriculum - often working with a teaching assistant through a set programme of activities. This might be seen as contradictory to **inclusive teaching**.

# INTRINSIC MOTIVATION

To be motivated by internal factors such as enjoyment or personal satisfaction.

# ADD ANY MORE DEFINITIONS YOU LEARN HERE...

# KEEPING CHILDREN SAFE IN EDUCATION (KCSIE)

The statutory guidance on safeguarding for schools, colleges and other educational institutions. Ofsted inspections always judge and comment on safeguarding processes and policies in schools.

## KEY STAGE 1 (KS1)

Years 1 and 2 in a **primary school** in England.

## KEY STAGE 2 (KS2)

Years 3–6 in a **primary school** in England.

## KNOWLEDGE ORGANISER

A document, usually no longer than one side of A4 paper, which sets out key facts and knowledge that children need for a unit of work for a specific curriculum subject.

# ADD ANY MORE DEFINITIONS YOU LEARN HERE...

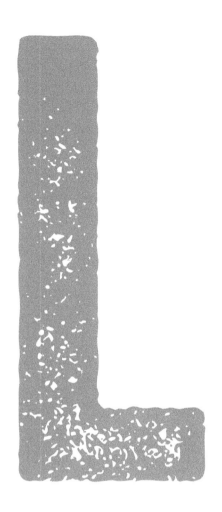

# LEARNING INTENTION (LI)

The focus for children's learning in the lesson, as set by the teacher in the lesson plan. Also referred to as the **learning objective** or **learning outcome (LO)**. Sometimes schools use other terms, such as **we are learning to (WALT)**.

## LEARNING OBJECTIVE/LEARNING OUTCOME (LO)

The focus for children's learning in the lesson, as set by the teacher in the lesson plan. Also referred to as the **learning intention (LI)**.

# LEARNING OUTSIDE THE CLASSROOM (LOTC)

Might refer to outdoor learning, or school outings or trips to places of interest or residential trips.

## LEARNING STYLES (ALSO REFERRED TO AS VAK)

An approach to teaching and learning that suggests that children favour a particular way of learning: e.g., visual, auditory or kinaesthetic. Although this idea has been popular in some schools, it has largely been discredited and has no scientific basis.

# LEARNING SUPPORT ASSISTANT (LSA)

An education support role. Often used interchangeably with **teaching assistant (TA)**.

## LEARNING THEORY

A way of understanding or explaining how learning happens.

# LESSON STUDY

A structured approach to **CPD** where teachers work together to address an identified area to develop in their children's learning.

It involves a cycle of improvement that includes collaborative planning of lessons, observation of the teaching of those lessons, group **reflection** and discussion and revision of the teaching. Lesson study continues over time rather than being a one-off event.

## LOCAL AUTHORITY (LA)

This is the overarching term for local government bodies such as county, district, borough or city councils. The LA will be responsible for delivering services such as education in the local area. The schools that work with the LA are called **local authority maintained schools**. **Academies** and **free schools** are independent of local authority control and receive funding direct from the government.

## LOCAL AUTHORITY DESIGNATED OFFICER (LADO)

The person in each local authority who is responsible for co-ordinating, managing and overseeing the response to concerns that an adult working with children may have or could cause them harm (see **safeguarding** and **child protection**).

## LOCAL AUTHORITY MAINTAINED SCHOOLS

**State schools** that are overseen by the local authority, from whom they receive funding and support. The local authority receives funding from central government, but it decides how to use this money to support the schools it has responsibility for.

Also known as maintained schools.

## LOOKED AFTER CHILD (LAC)

A child who has been in the care of a local authority for more than 24 hours. May also be referred to as a child looked after (CLA).

# ADD ANY MORE DEFINITIONS YOU LEARN HERE...

# MAINTAINED SCHOOLS

See **local authority maintained schools**.

# MASTER'S LEVEL (M LEVEL)

The academic level above the final year of a degree (level 7). Study at this level and above is called postgraduate study.

# MASTERY

A secure knowledge of a subject that can be adapted flexibly in a range of contexts. There is a particular emphasis on teaching for mastery in mathematics in primary schools.

# MEDIUM TERM PLANNING

See **scheme of work** and **unit of work**.

# MENTOR

In teacher education, the role of supporting but also assessing a **trainee/student teacher**. This is usually a school-based member of staff with experience of teaching and supporting teacher development. The mentor will work with external providers of ITE and **ITT** in order to deliver training and professional development and quality assure/moderate judgements made about the trainee/student teacher.

# META-ANALYSIS

See **systematic literature review**.

# METACOGNITION

Often described as thinking about thinking. Being aware of one's own thoughts and being in control of one's own thinking. This leads to a learner being aware of and understanding their learning behaviours and being able to make changes to those behaviours. Metacognition is often described as having two aspects: metacognitive knowledge (what learners know about learning) and metacognitive regulation (what learners do about their learning).

## MISCONCEPTIONS

Children's misunderstandings about basic concepts that might then affect their ability to develop understanding of more complex ideas. It is important that teachers design lessons taking into consideration what misconceptions might arise and identify and address misconceptions during teaching.

## MNEMONICS

A memory aid such as a rhyme or set of actions to help remember specific ideas or concepts.

## MODELLING

A pedagogical approach that involves teachers demonstrating to children the task or learning that they would like them to engage with (see **pedagogy**). This might include elements of **hidden curriculum** as well as a conscious approach to teaching.

## MODERATE LEARNING DIFFICULTIES (MLD)

A form of **special educational needs** that means a child is not attaining at expected levels despite support being in place.

## MODERATION

A process that looks across a set of assessments to ensure consistency of judgements/grading. See also **benchmarking**.

# MONTESSORI SCHOOLS

Follow an approach to teaching and learning based on the work of Maria Montessori. The focus is on developing children's instinctive learning, interests and activities through a carefully resourced environment, rather than through direct teaching instruction.

# MULTI-ACADEMY TRUST (MAT)

A charitable company, registered with Companies House, responsible for the operation of more than one **academy** school.

# MULTIPLE INTELLIGENCES

The idea that individuals might have particular personal strengths in different areas of the curriculum but that these are not recognised as 'intelligence' in the same way as is defined through, e.g., IQ testing. Based on work by Howard Gardner, this is a contested concept.

# MULTIPLICATION TABLES CHECK (MTC)

An online assessment of multiplication facts from the 2 to the 12 times tables for all Year 4 children in England. There are 25 questions. Children have six seconds to answer each question, with a three-second pause between each one. The check was announced in September 2017, but it did not become statutory until June 2022, after a pilot year and a delay due to the COVID-19 pandemic.

# ADD ANY MORE DEFINITIONS YOU LEARN HERE...

# NATIONAL CURRICULUM (NC)

The set curriculum taught in a particular country. The English national curriculum is statutory in state schools. There are different national curricula in Scotland, Wales and Northern Ireland.

# NATIONAL FOUNDATION FOR EDUCATIONAL RESEARCH (NFER)

An independent provider of educational research, generating evidence and insights at an international, national and local level.

# NATIONAL GOVERNANCE ASSOCIATION (NGA)

The official membership organisation for governors, trustees and clerks of state schools in England.

# NATIONAL PROFESSIONAL QUALIFICATIONS (NPQ)

Qualifications delivered by DfE selected providers to support the professional development of teachers and leaders. The qualifications cover leadership of others; leadership of a subject/year group, stage or phase; and leadership of behaviour/well-being of children.

# NATIONAL STANDARDS FOR SCHOOL-BASED INITIAL TEACHER TRAINING (ITT) MENTORS

A 2016 non-statutory document that sets out four broad mentor standards for school-based mentors who support **trainee/student teachers**.

# NEUROSCIENCE

The study of the brain and nervous system and how this relates to cognitive and behavioural development.

# ADD ANY MORE DEFINITIONS YOU LEARN HERE...

# OCCUPATIONAL THERAPIST (OT)

Assesses and supports children with physical and psychiatric needs. Will suggest and provide treatment to support children to become independent in the classroom.

## OFFICE FOR STANDARDS IN EDUCATION (OFSTED) (FULL NAME: OFFICE FOR STANDARDS IN EDUCATION, CHILDREN'S SERVICES AND SKILLS)

A government department responsible for the inspection of the quality of teaching and learning in schools and other education contexts in England.

# ORGANISATION FOR ECONOMIC CO-OPERATION AND DEVELOPMENT (OECD)

An international group that works to support policy development to enhance prosperity, opportunity and well-being across the world.

# ADD ANY MORE DEFINITIONS YOU LEARN HERE...

# PARENT TEACHER ASSOCIATION (PTA)

A voluntary organisation that supports a school with fundraising. Also known as the parents' association or 'friends of (the school)'. There is a National Confederation of Parent Teacher Associations (NCPTA).

## PASTORAL CARE

Support in school that is concerned with the welfare of students in terms of well-being rather than their academic achievements.

# PE AND SPORT PREMIUM FUNDING

Money given to non-independent primary schools from the government in order to make sustainable improvements to the quality of the PE, physical activity and sport they provide. Schools must publish on their websites how they use the funding.

## PEDAGOGY

A teaching approach based on a particular theoretical understanding of learning.

For example, social constructivist pedagogy would facilitate learning in groups in line with **social constructivism**.

'Chalk and talk' pedagogy is a **didactic** model that draws on the 'empty vessel' theory that the learner knows nothing and that learning happens when we are given the knowledge directly by a teacher. This would also be called a 'teacher-led' pedagogy.

'Child-centred' pedagogy is when the learning is led by the children through the choices they make within the learning environment. Lessons and teaching are planned based on assessments of the children's existing knowledge, skills and understanding. This approach comes from theoretical perspectives such as constructivism – we learn by building on what we already know and can do.

A skilful teacher is likely to draw on a range of pedagogies in their teaching as they adapt what they do to suit the needs of the learning task and the learners with whom they are working.

## PERFORMANCE (P) SCALES

Used to assess progress of children who have special educational needs and who have not yet reached level 1 of the **national curriculum**. From September 2021, P scales 1-4 were replaced by **the engagement model** and P scales 5-8 have been replaced by the **pre-key stage standards** for **Key Stage 1** and **Key Stage 2**.

## PERSONAL, SOCIAL, HEALTH AND ECONOMIC EDUCATION (PSHE)

A curriculum area designed to enable children to manage their lives and prepare them for life and work in the present and future. The **relationships and sex education (RSE)** curriculum is a statutory aspect of the wider subject area of PSHE. PSHE is a non-statutory subject.

## PHONEME

See **systematic synthetic phonics**.

## PHONICS SCREENING CHECK (PSC)

An assessment of Year 1 children to see how well they use their phonic knowledge to decode both real and non-words. They read a list of 40 words, with no time limit imposed. This happens in June.

## PHYSIOTHERAPIST (PT)

Works with children with physical disability or injury and suggests support to enable them to access education.

## PICTURE EXCHANGE COMMUNICATION SYSTEM (PECS)

Supports children's communication skills - pictures are used to enable a child to communicate with others.

# PLANNING, PREPARATION AND ASSESSMENT (PPA)

Teachers are entitled to this as part of their timetabled teaching time, as set out in the **school teachers' pay and conditions document**. This is usually ten per cent of the timetable but will be greater for **early career teachers** and pro rata for part-time teachers. Some schools allow teachers to use this time away from the school site. Teachers cannot be directed to undertake specific tasks during this time, and they should be reimbursed if the time is lost because of a school event. It cannot be reimbursed because of sickness or leave of absence.

## POSTGRADUATE CERTIFICATE IN EDUCATION (PGCE) OR PROFESSIONAL GRADUATE CERTIFICATE IN EDUCATION (PGCE)

An academic qualification awarded alongside QTS. This qualification is open to graduate students who hold a good first degree.

## PRE-KEY STAGE STANDARDS

In 2018, replaced P scales 5-8 for children with **special educational needs** who are working below **national curriculum** Key Stage 1 or Key Stage 2 standards - used to report outcomes for children up to Year 6.

See also **the engagement model**.

## PREPARATORY SCHOOLS

Fee-paying schools for children either aged 4-11/13 or 8-11/13 that prepare children to enter **public schools**. Also known as prep schools. Pre-prep schools are for children aged 2-7 or 4-7.

## PRE-SERVICE TEACHER

Someone following an **initial teacher training (ITT)** route to gain **qualified teacher status (QTS)**.

A term more commonly used outside the UK.

## PREVENT / THE PREVENT DUTY / THE PREVENT STRATEGY

Preventing people from being drawn into terrorism. Those working in educational settings, health and social care are required to know and be alert to indicators of extremism/radicalisation and it is mandatory to report concerns. There is online government training on prevent, which teachers are required to undertake.

## PRIMARY SCHOOL

Schools for children between the ages of 4 and 11 comprising of the **Reception class** and Years 1-6. All children will be aged 11 by the end of their final year of primary school.

## PRIVATE SCHOOLS

Privately owned **independent schools** that charge fees.

## PROFOUND AND MULTIPLE LEARNING DISABILITY (PMLD)

Children who have complex **special educational needs** arising from a range of disabilities.

## PROGRAMME FOR INTERNATIONAL STUDENT ASSESSMENT (PISA)

A study by the **OECD** that evaluates the performance of 15-year-old children in reading, mathematics and science through a test that is administered in member countries across the world every three years. Countries might use this data to inform education policies and improve outcomes.

## PROGRESS IN INTERNATIONAL READING LITERACY STUDY (PIRLS)

A study undertaken every five years by Year 5 children across more than 60 countries to assess children's reading skills, attitudes and motivation. The results are used to inform policy and practice and compare progress in reading across different countries. Administered by the International Association for the Evaluation of Educational Achievement (IEA).

## PROGRESS SCORES

A measure of each child's progress in reading, writing and mathematics between assessment points. See also **combined scores**.

## PUBLIC SCHOOLS

Elite **private schools** with very high fees.

## PUPIL PREMIUM (PP)

This is funding from government to improve education outcomes for disadvantaged children in schools in England. It is allocated to schools based on the numbers of children eligible for **free school meals (FSMs)**, **children in care (CICs)**, **looked after children (LACs)**/children looked after (CLAs), and children of members of the armed forces.

## PUPIL PROGRESS MEETINGS (PPM)

Meetings between teachers and a member of the **senior leadership team** to examine the data relating to the teacher's own class of children and their progress and attainment in relation to the whole school data.

## PUPIL REFERRAL UNITS (PRU)

Schools attended by children who need a mainstream school place but who might have been excluded from their usual school. They may also have missed school through illness.

# ADD ANY MORE DEFINITIONS YOU LEARN HERE...

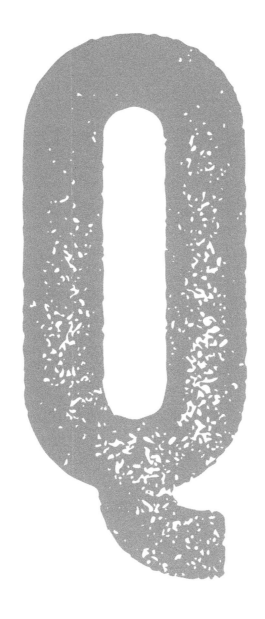

# QUALIFIED TEACHER STATUS (QTS)

A status awarded by the **teaching regulation agency** on completion of a recognised training course. It is a legal requirement to have QTS to teach in most schools in England. It is possible as a graduate to gain QTS without a further academic award such as a PGCE.

# ADD ANY MORE DEFINITIONS YOU LEARN HERE...

# RECEPTION BASELINE ASSESSMENT (RBA)

This is a statutory assessment that is undertaken within the first six weeks of the **Reception Year** and replaces the end of Key Stage 1 **standardised assessment tasks (SATs)** from September 2021.

# RECEPTION YEAR

Usually the first class in a **primary school** in England – children in Reception will be five years of age by the end of the academic year.

# REFLECTION

The way in which teachers think about their practice and development. They may do this more formally and systematically through the use of various models of reflection. Many of these models are used in health and social work as well as in teaching. Effective reflection enables analysis of what is happening/what has happened in order to improve. This allows teachers to be more proactive rather than reactive and builds confidence in their practice.

# REGIONAL SCHOOLS COMMISSIONER

Where a school is deemed to be underperforming, it will work with a regional schools commissioner to address the issues and improve outcomes. There are also national schools commissioners.

# RELATIONSHIPS AND SEX EDUCATION (RSE)

A compulsory subject area since September 2020. In primary schools, there is a focus on health and well-being, respectful relationships within the context of family and friends, and online relationships.

# REQUIRES IMPROVEMENT (RI)

One of four Ofsted inspection outcomes for schools along with outstanding, good and inadequate. Schools that receive this outcome will be provided with support and monitored so that they can move to either a good or outstanding judgement.

# RESEARCH

The process of finding out about something. This might be through reading about what other people say or it might be by systematically collecting evidence or data from a research project and offering an analysis of the findings (this is called empirical research). See also **action research**.

# RETRIEVAL

Recalling information when it is not in front of you. Some schools use retrieval practice to help children move information from their long term to their working memory.

# ADD ANY MORE DEFINITIONS YOU LEARN HERE...

# SAFEGUARDING

What is done for all children in order to keep them safe and to promote welfare. **Child protection** is part of safeguarding and promoting welfare. Every school has a **designated safeguarding lead (DSL)**.

# SCAFFOLDING

Using approaches and resources to support children to move forward independently in their learning; for example, writing frames, questioning, manipulatives. From the **social constructivism learning theory**.

# SCHEME OF WORK (SOW)

Medium term overview planning of a subject or a topic, setting out what is to be covered across a number of lessons and lasting a number of weeks. It may also include details such as assessments, resources, key learning, products, processes and timescale. Also referred to as a **unit of work**. Teachers/schools may create their own or purchase commercially produced schemes of work.

# SCHOOL-CENTRED INITIAL TEACHER TRAINING (SCITT)

Initial teacher training that takes place either wholly or largely within a school context. The trainee teacher will work in a school as a teacher while completing their training. They will be awarded **QTS** on completion of their training but will only be awarded a **PGCE** qualification if they have completed an academic course alongside their training.

# SCHOOL DEVELOPMENT PLAN

See **school improvement plan**.

# SCHOOL DIRECT (SD)

One of various routes into teaching. This is a graduate, school-led route where trainee teachers undertake their development with the majority of their time spent in school. It is run by a partnership between a lead school, other schools and an accredited teacher training provider. The trainee is either unsalaried (and therefore pays tuition fees) or salaried (and therefore is employed as an unqualified teacher).

## SCHOOL GOVERNING BODY

**Local authority maintained schools** all have a governing body. The governing body consists of volunteers from the local community, as well as having elected parent and teacher representatives. The governing body supports the head teacher in the work of the school and acts as a critical friend in the development of policies and practices as well as the general ethos of the school. The governing body is led by the **chair of governors**. In **academies**, the **academy trust** trustees perform a comparable role to the school governing body.

## SCHOOL IMPROVEMENT PLAN (SIP)

A plan that sets out the future of the school, including targets and actions to meet. The plan will identify any problem areas and how they will be tackled. Governing bodies/boards of directors will usually scrutinise these and monitor the plans, including how they are being put into effect and the impact on all stakeholders in a school. Ofsted will examine such plans but does not ask for them in any particular format. Sometimes called a **school development plan** or a **strategic plan**.

## SCHOOL TEACHERS' PAY AND CONDITIONS DOCUMENT (STPCD)

This is statutory guidance for **local authority maintained schools** and forms part of the contracts of the teachers who are working in these schools. It is updated annually.

## SCIENCE, TECHNOLOGY, ENGINEERING AND MATHEMATICS (STEM)

Education that promotes these four subjects or disciplines with a view to encouraging children to be more aware of and comfortable with them and the skills involved in engaging with them.

# SECRETARY OF STATE FOR EDUCATION

The cabinet minister in charge of the Education Department of the government.

# SECTION 28

A law that was in place between 1988 and 2003 that prevented teachers teaching that homosexual relationships were acceptable.

# SELF-EVALUATION FORM (SEF)

Schools use a SEF to evaluate current practices and processes and to identify areas for improvement. It then informs the **school improvement plan**. Ofsted does not require the SEF to be written in a particular format but will judge how appropriate and accurate the school's evaluations are and how they impact on practice and educational outcomes.

# SENIOR LEADERSHIP TEAM (SLT)

The teachers in a school who are responsible for leading the teaching team – might include the head teacher, year leads and subject leads. Might also be called the senior management team (SMT).

# SOCIAL CONSTRUCTIVISM

A **learning theory** that suggests learning is a social activity undertaken in interaction with others. Linked to **constructivism**.

# SOCIAL JUSTICE

The position that factors such as wealth, property, race and gender should not determine an individual's access to and engagement with education.

# SOCIO-ECONOMIC STATUS (SES)

An indicator of social standing – usually linked to income, education and occupation.

# SPACED PRACTICE

An approach to teaching that spreads out input and practice in particular information and concepts over time, rather than teaching it all in one go.

# SPECIAL EDUCATIONAL NEEDS (SEN) OR SPECIAL EDUCATIONAL NEEDS AND DISABILITY (SEND)

Refers to a range of needs that mean children require additional or specialist support to learn in school. This includes social or behavioural, cognitive and physical difficulties.

# SPECIAL EDUCATIONAL NEEDS CODE OF PRACTICE

Government produced guidance on the systems in place for supporting children with **special educational needs and disabilities**.

# SPECIAL EDUCATIONAL NEEDS CO-ORDINATOR (SENCO)

A teacher in a school who is responsible for co-ordinating the arrangements for children with special educational needs and disabilities.

# SPEECH AND LANGUAGE THERAPIST (SALT/SLT)

Works with children with **speech, language and communication needs** to enable them to communicate effectively. They will treat and assess children's needs and suggest support in the classroom.

# SPEECH, LANGUAGE AND COMMUNICATION NEEDS (SLCN)

The extensive range of needs relating to all aspects of communication. This is a broad category of need, including children with delayed language development and those with **developmental language disorder (DLD)**.

## SPELLING, PUNCTUATION AND GRAMMAR (SPAG)

See **grammar, punctuation and spelling (GPS)**.

# SPIRITUAL, MORAL, SOCIAL AND CULTURAL EDUCATION (SMSC)

Under this umbrella term, schools consider the personal development of all children across the curriculum. SMSC education is evaluated by Ofsted.

## STANDARD ENGLISH

Grammatically correct form of English, generally seen to be used in both spoken and written form by the educated. As part of the **teachers' standards**, a teacher must be able to demonstrate an understanding of and take responsibility for promoting the correct use of standard English.

# STANDARDISED ASSESSMENT TASKS (SATS)

Statutory tasks undertaken to assess children's progress against the **national curriculum** in English and maths. The compiled results of the tasks are published by the school. See also **reception baseline assessment**, **teacher assessment**, **grammar, punctuation and spelling**, **phonics screening check** and **multiplication tables check**.

## STANDARDS AND TESTING AGENCY (STA)

A government agency that develops the statutory standardised assessment systems used in **primary schools**.

## STATEMENT OF SPECIAL EDUCATIONAL NEEDS

See **education, health and care plan (EHCP)**.

## STATE SCHOOLS

Non-fee-paying schools that are largely government funded.

See also **private schools, independent schools, public schools, preparatory schools, academies, maintained schools**.

## STATUTORY

Required by law. Some aspects of teaching and teacher training are statutory requirements.

## STEINER SCHOOLS

Based on the ideas of Rudolf Steiner, these schools emphasise learning through play, imagination, creativity, art and physical movement.

## STRATEGIC PLAN

See **school improvement plan**.

## STUDENT TEACHER

Someone following an **initial teacher training** route to gain **qualified teacher status (QTS)**.

## SUBJECT KNOWLEDGE

The teacher's own knowledge of the subject(s) that they are teaching. It might also include knowledge in relation to the appropriate **pedagogy** for different subjects.

It is seen as an essential foundation for teaching and is specifically referenced in the **teachers' standards** as being part of the requirements for gaining **QTS**.

# SUCCESS CRITERIA (SC)

How a teacher and children judge the success of the intended learning in a lesson or a **unit of work**. Some schools choose to refer to the SC as **what I am looking for (WILF)**.

# SUMMATIVE ASSESSMENT

Usually tests or exams that are used to assess learning over a period of time, such as a unit of work, a term or a school year.

# SYSTEMATIC LITERATURE REVIEW

Gathers evidence from a range of research and synthesises the findings in relation to a particular question looking for patterns and themes. Also known as meta-analyses, meta-studies or systematic research reviews.

# SYSTEMATIC SYNTHETIC PHONICS (SSP)

An approach to teaching phonics that matches the individual sounds in words (**phonemes**) to letters (**graphemes**). This letter-sound relationship might be referred to as a **grapheme-phoneme correspondence (GPC)**.

# ADD ANY MORE DEFINITIONS YOU LEARN HERE...

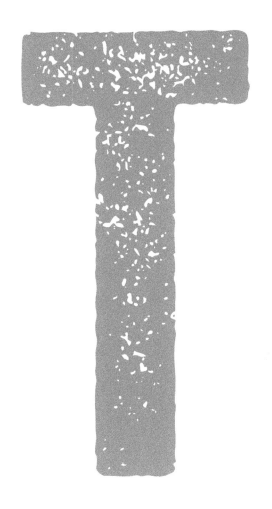

# TEACHER ASSESSMENT (TA)

May refer to teachers' **formative assessment** of children's work or **summative assessment** of children's work at the end of **Key Stage 1** or **Key Stage 2** undertaken alongside any statutory assessment tasks. Teacher assessment scores for writing at the end of Key Stage 2 are published alongside the statutory task outcomes.

## TEACHER REFERENCE NUMBER (TRN)

A unique number for each teacher that enables them to be identified by the **teaching regulation agency**. You are assigned a TRN when you embark on an **initial teacher training** course.

# TEACHERS' STANDARDS

Set out the expectations for teachers' performance and behaviour. Trainee teachers are assessed against the standards at the end of their **initial teacher training (ITT)**.

## TEACHING AND LEARNING RESPONSIBILITY PAYMENTS (TLR)

Payments that reward additional leadership and management responsibilities undertaken by classroom teachers.

# TEACHING ASSISTANT (TA)

An education support role working in the classroom. Often used interchangeably with **learning support assistant (LSA)**.

## TEACHING REGULATION AGENCY (TRA)

Has responsibility for overseeing the teaching profession, awarding **qualified teacher status**, dealing with teacher records and any misconduct hearings. It is a government agency sponsored by the **Department for Education**.

# TEACHING SCHOOLS

Schools that have been recognised for their excellent practice and support other schools' practice. This might be by providing **professional development** or specific support working one-to-one with individual schools. Teaching schools might also run a programme of school-based initial teacher training.

# TEACHING UNIONS

Work to protect the rights of teachers as well as providing support and guidance for individuals.

Some of the main teaching unions are:

National Association of Head Teachers (NAHT)

National Association of Schoolmasters and the Union of Women Teachers (NASUWT)

National Education Union (NEU)

# TEAM TEACHING (ALSO KNOWN AS CO-TEACHING)

Where two or more teachers purposefully and actively work together to share the teaching of knowledge and skills to children. This is more than the separation of sections of the lesson between teachers or other supporting adults.

# TRAINEE TEACHER

Someone following an **initial teacher training** route to gain **qualified teacher status (QTS)**. Also known as a **student teacher**.

# ADD ANY MORE DEFINITIONS YOU LEARN HERE...

# UNIT OF WORK

Medium term overview planning of a subject or a topic, setting out what is to be covered across a number of lessons and lasting a number of weeks. It may also include details such as assessments, resources, key learning, products, processes and timescale. Also referred to as a **scheme of work**.

# ADD ANY MORE DEFINITIONS YOU LEARN HERE...

# VISUAL IMPAIRMENT (VI)

A disability related to the ability to see.

# VOLUNTARY AIDED (VA) AND VOLUNTARY CONTROLLED (VC) SCHOOLS

A **state school** where the premises are wholly or partly funded by an organisation (usually religious). The organisation might also have an influence on the way the school operates. May also be known as 'church schools'.

# ADD ANY MORE DEFINITIONS YOU LEARN HERE...

# WALK THROUGH

Where the head teacher or a member of the SLT walks through the school/classrooms to look at the school environment and observe teaching in progress. Teachers will usually receive formal or informal feedback following a walk through and these might be announced in advance or be spontaneous. Might be linked to a **work/book scrutiny**.

# WE ARE LEARNING TO (WALT)

Some schools refer to the **learning intention (LI)** of a lesson in this way.

# WHAT A GOOD ONE LOOKS LIKE (WAGOLL)

Some schools use this to refer to a model text or an exemplification of any kind. This could be published/commercially available; written by the teacher or by a child.

# WHAT I AM LOOKING FOR (WILF)

How some schools talk about the **success criteria (SC)** of a lesson or **unit of work**.

# WHAT WENT WELL (WWW)

A marking comment that might be made on children's work to indicate where they have done well in a lesson. Often accompanied by **even better if (EBI)**.

# WORK/BOOK SCRUTINY

Looking at children's work to provide evidence as part of a judgement about the quality of the education provided. This is often undertaken in schools on a regular basis as part of an ongoing monitoring process. Ofsted inspectors scrutinise work during lesson observations and at other times in the inspection, to inform their judgement on whether children are making progress in knowledge, understanding and skills towards defined endpoints.

# WORKING AT THE EXPECTED STANDARD

Used in assessments to indicate children who are at the expected **national curriculum** standard at the end of the school year.

## WORKING TOWARDS THE EXPECTED STANDARD

Used in assessments to indicate where children have not yet met the expected **national curriculum** standard by the end of the school year.

# ADD ANY MORE DEFINITIONS YOU LEARN HERE...

# ZONE OF PROXIMAL DEVELOPMENT (ZPD)

From work by Lev Vygotsky. Suggests that there is a learning gap between what children can do independently and what they can achieve when supported by a 'more knowledgeable other'. **Scaffolding** is an approach to teaching that aims to support children to span the ZPD in their learning.

# 11-PLUS (11+)

A test undertaken by Year 6 children to gain entry to a grammar school. Not all areas have a selective system of secondary education, so this test will only be undertaken in some places.

# ADD ANY MORE DEFINITIONS YOU LEARN HERE...

# INDEX OF ACRONYMS